That Long Walk

That Long Walk

Femi Abidogun

Thynks Publications Limited

First published in 2015 by Thynks Publications Limited.

Registered Office:
White House, Clarendon Street, Nottingham, NG1 5GF England

http://www.thynkspublications.co.uk

Typesetting and Printing by
Book Printing UK
Remus House
Coltsfoot Drive
Woodston
Peterborough PE2 9BF

ISBN: 978-1- 900410-89-2

For
the ones who walked ahead of us
and showed us the way to go

PUBLISHER'S FOREWORD

To read a collection of poems by Femi Abidogun is to plunge into an ocean of deep and sensitive thoughts and feelings. He shares his experiences as well as carefully observing them.

The first poem in the collection – *A Day Like any Other* bursts upon the reader with a kind of blessing and is a reminder to be thankful and grateful for each day of our lives.

When disconcerted by life events and observations historically and currently, globally and personally, he searches positively for a way through and via poetry.

It is a sheer pleasure to read the poems written with such tenderness and affection, for and about his wife. The genuineness with which he honours her shines through.

He deals with a multitude of subjects and with a certain wisdom. Sometimes he is prosaic and sometimes he slides into rhyme and rhythm both subtly and blatantly, wherever the words seem to take him. The title poem takes this collection to another level, not just for now but for the future and for global significance; not just as a personal reflection but as a collective view, with the tribute to Nelson Mandela.

PREFACE

That Long Walk, my second collection of poems, is coming on the heels of my previous anthology, *Blonde Grass*. However, it is a bigger collection of poems with even more diverse themes.

Over the last two or so years preceding its release, we have witnessed the passing of the inspirational Nelson Mandela as well some of the most talented writers of our time. As such, some of the poems featured in this anthology have been written as tributes in their honour.

I would like to appreciate the invaluable contributions of *Thynks Publications* and Christine Michael in making this work a reality. My gratitude to them also for allowing some of my poems which had previously appeared in the *Bards at Blidworth and Beyond* anthologies to be included in this collection. Many thanks also to Pam Brindle for painstakingly going through the work despite her busy schedule.

Finally, a huge thank you to my wife Victoria (Titi), my girls-Mosope and Tamilore, my parents, and my siblings Deola, Fola, Deji and Nike for their ever-present love, inspiration and support.

Femi Abidogun

CONTENTS

A DAY LIKE ANY OTHER

Today,
There appears
Out here,
A sight rare.
Rousing in the air.
Seemingly here
Is a great abundance
Of unparalleled radiance;
The golden sun is out smiling
Leaving everywhere
Bright and shiny
The sky is as bright as can be
So for a change, we do no whining
The only sounds to our hearing
Are birds in flight chirruping
In an atmosphere very inspiring.
As this day grows by
Ageing gracefully into a gleaming night
An aftermath of the full moon's cheery light,
We look left, right
And then up high
Deep into the sky's eyes
In the quest to know why
It's such an ennobling day.
Just then, the murmurings of calm, therapeutic breeze
Silence us and say:
True, it is a beautiful day
But every single day
In its own little way
Is one

Just bask in it without further delay
For every waking day
Is a glorious one
We are just too blind
To see it
Too proud
To acknowledge it
Too ungrateful
To recognise it
Too busy
To spare that all-important second appreciative look.

A DREAM MERELY CRACKED

Shattered
Like a broken glass' shards
Flung wide and far
After an inglorious fall
From a dizzying height
Scattered
Like wandering nomads
Far, near and all around
In a quest for a guaranteed survival
Hammered
Like one forced to eat the humble pie
Served
With a generous portion
Of the requisite remorse
But still with one eye open
Waiting to seize the next opportunity
To rise again
And hopefully stay up
Never to fall again.

A FEW KIND WORDS

A word
Walks a mile
A kind one
Or perhaps two
Could carry some
Thousands of miles.
She uttered a few
And I smiled
As I flew
From the bottom
To the very top
Of this world.

AORTA

Free my heart en-shackled
Like a sprawling *Gothic* castle
Re-captured after a successful battle.
Without this, there'd be even more hassles
And my lonesome heart will stay embattled
Till you rush here to get it startled
And make it pop alive like a vintage champagne bottle.

ATOP THE NIGER

As your swerving currents sway
My unsettled mind strays
From here to many miles away
Seeking the right way
That's best before I call it a day.
It hovers and plays
And rustles endlessly like your restless waves
Looking for where to berth
Like those vessels that transverse your path
In their bid to reach home before night is past.
It desires your rare calmness
In the dry season
When your waters almost run dry
And stills the likelihood of turbulent waves.
It longs to be tranquil
Like your marine life
Relatively unperturbed despite the many ills
Caused you by man and his ilk.
It seeks to hold on fast
To whatever riveting ideas that may pass
Hoping this would suffice
To make my head easily lie.
I need to make my head
As clear as your waters
Which are devoid of much silt;
It needs to be rid
Of as much past regrets and guilt
And move on as rapidly
As your waters daily flow speedily.

AUSTERITY

Sullen faced
As they surface
Heading to that same old place
Dragged like the previous case
With virtually no say.
Off to the stream of economic strangulation
The one badly in need of depuratives
To neutralise its harshness
The same one held in dread
Not just for its depths
Nor its tumultous waves
But because like before
They are again forced to dip into it
Their rusting, sinking vessels
And taste the usual sourness
That leaves rancid after-tastes
Which stubbornly remain
And refuse to vanish given its unwelcome pain.

BEFORE OUR VERY EYES

Before our very own eyes
Lived Nelson, a man with numerous great deeds
Unlike many before and after him
Moved many a mountain and hill.
Before our very own eyes
He crossed countless hitherto impassable seas
Building bridges
Over and beyond just what our naked eyes could see.
Compared to many of his peers,
He was ahead by light years
Shining brightly like a constellation of stars
Just like a rare gem or pearl.
To many he was more than just their pal
Desired by all
Adored by more.
Before our very eyes
Alas, we have seen
The very one that showed us
What true greatness really means.
Not ever likely
Will there ever be
Any other close enough
To be like him
So let us be glad,
And be jubilant
For what our eyes have seen.

BLIND AT DAMASCUS

Thankfully it is not
But then it could easily have been any one of us
On the vexed streets of *Aleppo, Homs* or *Damascus*
Rendered homeless
Fleeing,
Feeling hopeless –
Innocent ones
Caught up in the deadly crossfire of a conflict needless,
Battling hunger, strife and an uncertain fate
Staring adversity
So very hard in the face
Living everyday as an unenviable nightmare
Dreaming today would quickly go away
Fearing what tomorrow may bring its way
Wondering if there's any end in sight
Asking why the world watches as it looks the other way
Yes, wondering
If the world has lost its very own sight.

CHILD'S PLAY

I see smiles light up
Their young, dimpled façades
Though I perceive hunger
Clobbering them with its *knobstick*.
Their intermittent giggles
Get run over by rumbling tummies
Which have learnt to hum hardly-sonorous tunes;
Tunes which speak of their being held as captives of starvation.
I see all pairs
Of popped-up stares
Firmly transfixed in the same pathway
Tempting one to surmise
That perhaps a spell has been cast
To make steady those gazes.
I see signs
Of excitement as *Barney* and friends surface from nowhere;
Followed afterwards by *Tom* fiercely chasing *Jerry*
And later, *Peppa Pig* jumping in muddy puddles.
I see mama stroll in,
Armed with motherly entreaties
Desiring to put a break to it
But without much luck.
I finally see
The reason for all these
And discover the great conjurer
Is not a seasoned magician,
But simply just the screen!

CROSSWORDS

The tone may be darker
Or the tint may be brighter
But no matter the way it's looked at
Deep inside
It's still the one primary colour.
The goal posts have moved
With the old players removed
But surely the style remains the same
Still the one game.
The dam is full
The same quantity of water stilled
No drop more nor any less
But it isn't an ocean still.
The skin appears dry
May look a bit pale
Seems at times covered in scales
But the leopard's spots stay the same.
For deep-seated
Deeply ingrained
Not looking like some things will ever change
Or be any less different perhaps till...

        ...peacocks shed their colours
      ...games are without laws
     ...the oceans run dry
       ...leopards appear in stripes
      ...and the spoken word
       is uttered with absolutely no words

DARING DREAM

As this night slowly slips
And we stubbornly stay away from sleep
Counting not innumerable sheep
But the sky's many stars as they continually dip
And watch the half moon reluctantly recede
While dreaming dreams with eyes wide ajar
Promise that you'll do this with me
Not just this night
But again and again
Till we count down to the very last meteor
And our dreams are for real

DEW DROPS

We come
We see
And we get
Together

We wail
We wave
And then
Go Away

Next, we write
And barely wrote
And don't write
Right now

...nor any more!

DIAMONDS ARE FOREVER

Shone like a glistening
diamond;
Like a gold fish shimmering
in a dreary pond.
Though not with us any longer,
Madiba's legacies linger
And will continue to guide and glitter
Like the rare gem
He and his works truly are
To you, I, us and them.

DREAM TEAM

A queen you seem
Since in my heart you reign
Supreme.
Its inmost chalét you should see
As your palace and the home of dreams
Made of the finest gilt
Painstakingly refined in
Furnaces of the fond thoughts
You always bring.
Your graceful charm ignites
Fireworks of delight.
Even with all these
I don't have to be a king
Having all the powers that be
Nor even a prince
With serfs waiting on me.
All I need
Is being content with
Just anything that will keep
You being my very own queen.

DRIED INK

(For Chinua Achebe, Seamus Heaney,
Maya Angelou and Nadine Gordimer)

The ink may blurt
Causing a few to hurt
Its drops may dry up
Needing many more to cheer up
The pen may altogether stop
Leaving us all worse off
It may even go missing
Never ever to be seen
But the manifold offspring
In the form of great works
Great words
Wonderfully strung
Continue to bloom like many a spring's
Daffodils that continually sprung

EBOLA

As we looked on undecidedly
Thinking it's never a big threat
As long as it's the other's problem.
Watching with hands akimbo
Feeling that by doing nothing, you will just go
Dilly-dallying like an unsure bambino
Contemplating his very first steps.
You decimated faster than wild bush fires
Seasonally on the go.
You infected legions, orphaning thousands
Stinging harder than a spiteful bee
Overwhelming like an overflowing deep-sea
Leaving on your trail
Misery, doom and pain
And questions seeking to see
If a respite to all this
There'll ever be
And who the next victim may turn out to be.

EDGE OF HOPE

This night is expectant
Just like an almost due mater.
So at the twilight
Of tonight,
In the labour room
Of unrelenting hope,
On the shores
Of promise,
A better tomorrow
Will hopefully berth
As the progeny of this much anticipated birth.

EIGHTEEN AGAIN

A year
Older –
Is all
That's said;
It's all
Just a thing
Of the mind –
We heard that too before;
Age
Is only
A number –
It's always asserted;
But in this case
What exactly
Is this
Figure?

EUREKA

I once eagerly sought
That one dart
That would aim perfectly
Right.
For what
Seemed like aeons
I slaved as time's serf on and on
Waiting for heaven's silver bullets.
Sweat
And tears welled
Up till my ducts swelled
But still
I let the waters rise
Staving off
The very idea of
Falling for tinselled joys
That arrive today and are tomorrow gone.
All said and done
The wait
Is not all
In vain
Since after all the toil
It's now *eureka*
For I eventually found you.

FILLING THE GAPS

You may be there
Miles away from where I'm sat
Worn by tears, fears,
Spaces and gaps,
Built up over the years,
But what we share
Is definitely bigger
Than the chasm that seem to appear.

FOOD FOR THOUGHT

How can we grab
Any more delicious grub
When our tummies churn
With morsels of disgust
At others being famished and hurt?

Are we not forced to spew
The bit we have chewed
By their depressing sights
In food scavenging hunts
Even in the midst of waste?

Do we sleep
When our eyes so often see
Images of strife
Or just sigh and wonder 'what a life?'

Do our hearts bleed
Pints of guilt
When with so many around
Help is nowhere near
Or at best mere drops in a mighty body of water?

Where is our gaze centred
Now that it is needed in one direction
That one eagerly needing our timely action
To avoid irreversible consequences of our inaction
That will require even more efforts
Than if we just pause now and for once sort?

FORGETTING TOMORROW

All have now forgotten
They've ever eaten
Even the drinks taken
Have dried up completely
The drums have stopped beating
The participants exhausted and tired
The hitherto high tunes wane so the dance moves expire
And the once-deafening applause
Till another day paused
What follows is continual hissing
And discontent with the status quo
Plus the dawning on all present
Of a dingy reality that is persistent
Temporarily forgotten but still very much prevalent
Reminding all
Of how they ate, drank and danced off
Revelling in the now
Watching the stomach momentarily alter its structure
In lieu of tangible, long-lasting infrastructure
While a thought for the future
Didn't for once feature
But only occupied the back burner
Waiting endlessly in vain
For common sense to at least prevail

FORTY

It hadn't been without flaws
From those early little crawls
To the massively huge course
All through, so exhaustively busy
And things at some point didn't look like easing.

It sure didn't come on a platter
Without its own fair share
Of us running helter-skelter
Just like bread being plastered
With unyielding, coagulated butter.

The road was bumpy
Many times even stumpy
With journeys that have been rocky
Littered with obstacles thrown from all parts,
Frequently wondering if there'd ever a respite.

But you have always prevailed
Come rain or shine
No matter the clime
The day always seemed
To end with a beaming smile.

For in all these
Through all these
You removed the fears
Making things easier to bear
Even where there seemed to be no thoroughfare.

So what more can one do
But to stay grateful?
Allow you go on helping to pull through,
Put further trust deeper in you,
And hold on tight to you,
Never ever to let go
For life has only just begun.

FROZEN

It is cold out here – oh yes, it really is
And I feel the same chill
As that on a wintry night atop a *Siberian* hill
But oh no,
I do not mean the severity of the sub zero
Which leaves the atmosphere in blight
Or that which has before on many nights
Left us all frozen with frost bites.

It isn't either
The kind of cold that's the ineluctable effect
Of several hours' ceaseless
Outpouring of snowflakes
Landing on my thick kinky hair
Like a *Boeing* laid bare
As it flies straight from the air
Onto the tarmacs of *Heathrow*, *Schiphol* or *O'Hare*.

I feel the cold
And it's that sort
That makes me go
Wishing I had several layers of skin
To make not just my bones
But me as a whole
Hang on
For just a little bit more.

It's the peculiar cold that's evolved
From the dearth of familiar words
That our ears itch to hear.
It's that cold which I find ensconced
In the plentiful supply of unacquainted reticence.
It is the iciness from tittle-tattle when backs are turned
And the coldness of the scowling giggles
Which trail dialect-laden voices.

It's that frostiness emanating from glaciated smiles
That barely scratch the surface of genuine concern.
It's the cold oozing from frozen acts of doubts;
Of 'can anything good come from *l'etranger*'.
It is the cold from the void.
Of the separation and distances felt away on the road
It is these that have had many hit by their icy spears.

This cold seems too bad for one
So I hunger not just for the blistering *Saharan* sun,
But also for the heat from the engaging and loud laughter
During those never to be forgotten, never-ending banters.
I long for warm, soothing familiar words
Many miles away from this part of the world,
Across several seas,
To light the fire that can quench this burning chill.

I thirst for those warm reassuring countenances
To melt away the ice from stony, rock hard grimaces
That often make me wonder if I'm from *Jupiter* or *Mars*.
I desire those overdue hugs and warm embraces
To heat the gelidity of separation and kept distances.
I yearn for the warmth of motherland to lessen this cold
And make me feel like I just struck gold
Many many many miles away from home.

HELPLINE

If iron can be wringed
So much squeezed
That it drips
Like cheap ink

If oceans
Chose
A language other than those
Only blue waters spoke

If only the emu
Could leap high
And take a hike
Across the massive white skies

Then I won't
Be here
Putting blue ink
On off-white paper

HOMESTRETCH

I have reached my harbour
After some real hard labour
Though others may journey on with even more ardour.
My ship had set sail
Tried not to derail
And has now finally hit land.
The piers have stayed firm
I am home and dry,
And I've dropped the anchor
About to step onshore.
The time to disembark
Has ultimately arrived
For the search for love
Seem to have ended
The moment I met you.

HUES OF UHURU

I perceive no choking, polluting miasma
Coercing me
To desperately wait to exhale

I see no frenzied sights
Billowing to the rooftop
An already exasperated fortitude

I hear no disconcerting clatters
Strangulating pitilessly
A wearied forbearance

I feel no jerky pressures
Tormenting ceaselessly
My frayed, berserk nerves

I perceive whiffs from the ancestral forests
Awakening me
To its intrinsic beauty

I see calm rivulets
Mirroring lush greenery
With the words verve and serene spluttered all around

I hear cute whistling birds
Sonorously chirping
Melodies of tranquility and liberty

I feel warmth
Tagged with acceptance
In the soothing embrace of Blidworth.

HUNDRED DEGREES

Filled to the brim
Is the gourd of patience in him.
It drips
And runs over the mill
Courtesy of his adversaries' increasing heat;
Multifarious cracks emerge about it –
The aftermath of a surfeit
Of insults he did not merit.
Now the bubble's burst
With the die firmly cast –
The once placid gentleman
Is given an goaded makeover
Into some stroppy,
Grumpy,
Mean old chap.

I CLOSE MY EYES

I close my eyes
When I look at you
So I can see you
The way you truly are
I don't wanted to be blinded
By sights obscuring the real you
Nor by flashy garbs, drab robes
Or paraphernalia that may or may not
Make you glow.
With my eyes closed, I open my ears
And listen hard
To the words you have carefully uttered
So I may hear their true depths loud and clear
Not paying attention
To the vagaries of the exotic intonation
Instead sieving out the messages embedded
And appreciating the import of facts stated.
I open my arms with my eyes well shut
Spread so wide till they are broad
Enough to hold you and any other
Who desperately desire or seek a big hug
Irrespective of how roundly or not
My outstretched hands wrap round them
No matter how thick or thin their skin is.
I close my eyes
When I look at you
So that I see you
Only the way I wish
You and every other will see me.

IRONY OF A CON-DOCTOR

Ten minutes drilled
Into the new hour's till
Yet like freezing ice
We still chill.
Ah finally to a halt
A bus stills
'*Bustop Gate! Gate Buststo*p'
The conductor calls
We get thrilled
And then shudder
At the sound of that distinctively familiar voice;
That which belonged to a former school mate
Who in those good, old days
Referred to himself as 'Doctor'
But we find him this moment,
A bus conductor!

MANIFESTO OF LOVE

Shine that burning flame
I won't do a thing to get it tamed.
Broach your feelings right to the last
I'm all eager to have them shared.
Never be afraid to drop a tear
I'll mop it with utmost care.
And regarding towers to lean on?
On my shoulders you're forever welcome.
Never ever say never
For you all is possible always ever.
Fret not over battles yet to be won
For my love will eventually conquer all.

MELANCHOLY

I am at
The downturn
Of the billows
Deep down
Where the ebb
Is really low
Down-swings are all
That there are
But while down here
As I lay
In this rough trough
I wait for you
To lift me up
And turn this burst
Once again
Into a boom

MIRAGE

Jackpot
I thought
Then I jumped
And get the bright tarred patch thumped
As I incessantly rejoiced
Only to find out
It wasn't yet *uhuru*
For the glow
Of the dim beacon
That seemed to beckon
Waned
And suddenly began to fade
Into oblivion
On and on
Leaving me
Marooned
Back to my lonely, cold room
To lick the wounds
Of blistered expectations
And bruised aspirations.

MONA LISA

A master piece he drew
With the sky's blue
Differing in its hues.
Sprightly too,
The flowers bloom
Giving it an altogether scenic view;
Another *Mona Lisa* looms
Yet still nowhere
Close to
Being as beautiful
As you.

NIGHTBEAT

Shhhhhhhhhhhhh!
The delicate sheath
Of quiet
Stays
Unbroken tonight
Very much unlike
The regular night
When nebulous noises erupt
All around and about.

Not like those nights when the crisp rustles
Of crunchy leaves
Contend with
Rusty frog-croaks
Or yelling cry-babies
Who squeal
And squeak
To jostle awake
Their ever-pliant mothers.

This night is wearied
By the usual;
So the roaches, tonight, roam
Stealthily.
Swishing hisses
Are barely heard,
And the ubiquitous
Creepy crawlies
Slouch serenely.

Alas
Our exaltation
Is rendered premature;
The frail pane of peace
Is shattered
No thanks
To the neighbourhood night-watchman
And the emphatic shrill din
Emanating from his goofy gong
Heralding the old man's
Report to duty
Supposedly to keep the peace.

NOSTALGIC

Back under the ageless almond tree
Reminiscing
Wishing
The chimes
Of a distant time
Would re-sound over again
And the seasons
Long gone could have re-runs
Such that the senescent almond tree
Could once more drop its 'fruits'
On our coconut heads
And reinstate the good old days
That then
In our childish eyes
Just didn't seem good enough.

ON BENT KNEES

Truly for real
There may not be
A land solely
Made of just dreams

Life may even seem
To all
To be
Everything but fairy dreams

But still
If you will
My heart's fate
You sure can redeem

Make it not bleed
So take heed
Of me
And my most earnest plea

That by my hand you take me
And step in
This moment
And walk evermore with me

ONE LAST DANCE

When did time rush by
Stealthily gushing by
Like the waters of the *Niagara*
Hastily, away it ran
Several autumns have replaced reluctant summers
Many a warm spring have seen the rear
Of bitterly, chilly winters;
Through numerous rainy seasons to dry seasons
We have wasted enough time seeking reasons
Needed action to back words we were used to speaking
Seem the link conspicuously missing.

Where did all the time go
Disappearing like a piteous object in a magic show –
Now you see then you don't.
But before any more decide to go
We need to get on a new boat –
That vessel of a new resolve
And row, row and row
Putting everything we need in tow
Shrugging off the old wild waves that hinder the flow

Before the waters run dry
And again put progress on hold
Before the weather gets too cold
Before we all grow too old.
The journey to mending our cracked dreams must begin
Rediscovering it
Before it becomes
A totally broken dream.

So with a generous dose of requisite valour
Like a perpetual suitor
Seeking to impress
Ready to take his chance
Asking yet again for another dance
We rise
Dusting off ourselves
To begin afresh
On a path of uncovering
A new beginning
Hoping that this time we get it right
Like that suitor who's saved his best moves
Once given what may well be a final chance
For that very last dance.

ON MY WAY TO PICCADILLY

Headaches,
Backaches,
Leg aches
And all kind of pains.
Hearts aching,
Bellies aching.
Banging,
Clanging noises.
Haggling,
Arguing,
Haranguing voices
That seem somewhat cracked,
Ad-mixed
With a cacophony of clattering tracks;
Ageing, rusty, noisy tracks.
Three, four or five
Extra-ordinarily chatty chaps
In unfettered, not-so-smattering chats
Lousily,
Loudly,
Largely
With seemingly uncontrollable traps.
Everyone here
Is either
A victim
Or culprit
We are all in it together;
Yes, cramped together in it;
This contraption generating quite some heat.

I see
Lovers without cold feet
Holding hands,
Suitors staring hard
Onlookers watching by
Many looking sad
Some feeling bad
A number slouch by
Others jump in
Fearing
Not to be stranded and left behind
Score of faces simply gazing
Others friendly,
A few smiling,
Some stony,
One or two very blank
Just too queer
To clearly decipher.
Everyone rushing somewhere
But some, exactly nowhere
Frequent, frenzied stopping
Almost as quickly as the take-off
Finally it stalls
As it abruptly halts
And suddenly
I see there's light
At the end
The very end of this tunnel.

PHOTOSHOP

On the wall of a warm, brightly-lit room
Beclouded by not an iota of gloom
Ostensibly, just elegance looms
It brings an atmosphere dignified
Which many had always said it signified
But at the back of the face-lifting mask of mascara
Beyond the film of a solemn mien
Behind the veil of plastic smiles
And beneath the façade of a calm face
Lies a soul restless,
Often relentless
In its craving for true happiness –
Genuine joy that traverses just grins
Crying out to anyone with eyes discerning
To please
Reveal what genuine peace
Actually is.

RISKY BUSINESS

Not circumspectly
I lurk
And get firmly
Locked
Around the peaceable space
Of gentle inertia
Yielding
To her primordial appeal
Of perpetuating
The status quo

Suddenly
I retrace my steps
Though I wish
I just won't cease
But I need to brash
And perhaps a little brisk
Taking this projected risk
Possibly losing my face
In your very own eyes
And see
My stature shrink

But
Who knows
The skies
May stay the same
And not fall
Just yet or perhaps at all

THAT LONG WALK

No one could tell exactly how far he'd go
When, long ago
He was born in *Mvezo*;
Not too many even knew
The next couple of years at *Qunu*
Would be the necessary early steps
Of that extraordinary trek
An extended journey he had started,
A century shy of five it eventually lasted.

A travel filled with ups, downs and hardships untold,
As he tread through paths previously un-towed;
Roads that made him tell the world
That it always seems impossible until it's done;
That the greatest glory in living
Lies not in never falling,
But in rising every time we fall,
And that one was still imprisoned
If hatred and bitterness were still harboured.

A victor, an emancipator,
A true leader, an inspiration
And a path finder for us all
And for anyone
Who truly desires to know how to carry on,
Despite numerous hurts
And innumerable pitfalls –
Taught us to work hard, persevere,
Give, forgive and get the move on.

Now gone via *Qunu* –
The early homeland he once knew
Having fully paid his own dues
Madiba, to you, we continually say thank you
As you take a deserved bow
From what was more than just a short promenade;
To you we have also had our goodbyes bade
Celebrating your freedom from that long, exhaustive,
But ultimately, rewarding walk.

THE BEAUTIFUL ONES

The beautiful ones
Are not yet unborn
For they've long been born
And are far gone
While we looked away
Expecting angels draped
In satin and suede
Bringing power, glitter and fame
While we got carried away
Delusions and fantasies played
Leaving us acting like we had no brains.

The beautiful ones have long walked away
While we got carried away
Swept off our feet by
Grand illusions that never see the light of day
The beautiful ones didn't seem pretty enough
So we didn't realise they were the very ones
As if we ourselves were merely
An inch from being paragons
For vanity and sophistry
Strongly held sway.

So never should we say
The beautiful ones are yet to be born
For by our free will we chose the other way
Even while they were here and with us stayed
Now that the beautiful have long been born
And too many miles from our reaches far away
Who would we resort to rescue us and save the day?

THE BULLRING

You are calmly sitting
Like a gracious heart filled with pity
You rest majestically at the very heart of the city
And are acclaimed for your unique ability
Of providing unrivalled therapy – retail therapy
Once we've got our cards, wads of notes or loads of 50ps
But tell me; what is it about you that exerts the pull
Which gets people trooping in, making this arena full
Here, there and around your imposing bronze bull?
Hundreds, possibly, thousands of passers-by
Ceaselessly besiege you and drop by
Some just to catch the bull's eyes.
Others go shop-hopping, hoping to eventually find
Either the perfect price or that right size.
But many end up with deep sighs
Bewildered, they wander
And wonder
About what and where best to buy.
Others simply window-shop and say good-bye
After sufficiently feeding their hungry eyes.
First timers, long-timers and indeed all
No one ever fails to get enthralled
As enticed shoppers flock into your huge shopping halls
That impress and make *Brum* stand tall.
Many stroll into your cafes, restaurants and bistros,
In and around, hordes form unending queues and rows
Just to give themselves a real treat.
But finally, there is a retreat
For you there's a sigh of relief
As the sun gives way to the moon
And many tired and burdened with bags of their boon
Vestiges of their shopping boom
Begin to depart like litter being swept off by a broom.

They stream past your running bronze bull
That stays and remains ever static.
As they glide down your slopes and go by *St Martin*
They hear the ringing of its bells starting
Making a clarion call to the wearied and heavy laden
To come in and forever lay down their burden.

*The Bullring is one of the busiest shopping centres in the United Kingdom and attracts shoppers from all over the world. Located at the end of its slopes is the St Martin Church.

THE WORLD IS ROUND

The world is round
It spins around
From here to there
It does not begin nor end
At only your homestead
Though I know that instead
You've always thought it a mere triangle
Where all is seen only from your angle
Where good things only dangle
When hoisted on platforms only you are entangled
Or perhaps you even thought of it as a square
Seeing everything as yours alone never to be shared
But that wouldn't be just or even considered fair.
For the world is round
It rolls on and on,
End to end, non stop
Knocking on everybody's door
Proving that every soul counts.

TONGUE-TIED

I swam
Through the vast seas
Of words
Hoping I'll find the one
That perfectly captures you.
Like a coiffeur
I frantically combed.
Combing through the hairs
Of semantics
Thinking a chestful of apt words
Describing you, I'll find.
As a vigilant ranger would
On the look out for clues
I snooped around
Seeking to have you unwound
And find comprehension
All in my determined bid to fully grasp you.
These are in vain
For not one find
Is good enough
To depict appropriately
That awesome wonder
That you just are.

VOICE OF SILENCE

When the mouth grows heavy
It feels like twelve years in slavery,
Or someone who's had a hundred years of solitude.
It could feel like a lady
Laden
With so much emotional burden.
The tongue
Acts like it's glued
Like a political prisoner fettered with no clue
Of when he would be freed.
Battered lips stay sealed
Hence nothing revealed
Except a consequent despair and lack of zeal.
Simple words
Are locked up in another world –
A new realm of unwanted silence
Away from where they should announce a big presence.
Another era of playing deaf and dumb
Is a new reborn.
Words become the forgotten prisoners;
The victims who ultimately lose
Waiting to be let loose
From the chains of their captors
While hoping to have a further day to live
And hopefully be set free
Seriously itching to make that major difference
Between the consequence
Of some home truth spoken
And that of a silence kept forever.

WET BLANKET

They always say
What a wry face
And also claim
The pace
Is a tad too drawn-out;
A laughing stock
Every effort is contorted into
While the outcome too
Don't get any treatment better
Just as whispers
Race after
Every try.
Never good enough
Is always the verdict
As their dismal curtains of cynicism
Are drawn to a relieving close
Albeit temporarily
For soon, there'll be a replay
Of all these once again
Much to my indifference
As I'll carry on, still
With replenished zeal
As if oblivious
Of my detractors' distractions
Till the Red Sea is crossed
And the hill's peak is reached.

WINDOW SHOPPING

Her lean purse stays famished
So she's again banished
And left to strut and catwalk
Not inside the High Street shops
But on the side-walk;
Relegated to just feeding her eyes
On the alluring stock
Enticingly displayed behind
The translucent windows and glass
While anxiously waiting for her wallet
To be stuffed once again
And hoping the flattening of her pocket wanes
Sooner than much later.

WORDS ARE NEVER ENOUGH

E seun,
For every tread of my journey, tightly sewn
Be it zigzag, patched up or straightly hewed
Till fit and befitting
For whatever realm
Was my loosely running helms.
Nagode,
For every tear for me dropped
Just to save and stash away my own tear drops.
Dalu,
For turning things around when things looked
Like all I would ever get was just boos
Or at best from cows some moos
Merci,
For your sweaty beads that relentlessly dripped
Till of myself I got an overdue grip.
Danke,
For every supplication for me muttered
As you perched on knees bruising and knackered.
Obrigado,
For your foraying eyes that ran amok
Tracing my faltering steps
Till they steadied like *Olumo rock.*
Asante,
For unwavering, seemingly blind faith
In believing that no matter what
I will get the best of fates
Shukran,
For your countless acts of deprivations
Just to ensure my own constant provision
Gracia,
For being my shadow's constant rival
On each step of unknown roads I chartered

Shukhriya,
For staying on
As others ran
While the rain poured till again
The sun shone
Xie xie,
For always being there
Whether I'm far away or even just here.

...no matter what ways I try
Or how hard I strive
I cannot enough thrive
In my search for the right choice of words
and my heartfelt bid to sufficiently say
a really huge thank you!

"Whether you turn
To the right
Or to the left,
Your ears will hear
A voice behind you
Saying:
This is the way;
Walk in it"

Isaiah 50 : 21